USES for MOOSES
and other popular pets

BY
MIKE THALER
ILLUSTRATED BY
JERRY SMATH

WHISTLESTOP ®

Troll Associates

In memory of
Milton Polinsky,
friend and neighbor—
M.T.

For my sisters-in-law,
Frances, Letitia, and Roberta.
Love, J.S.

Library of Congress Cataloging-in-Publication Data

Thaler, Mike.
Uses for mooses and other popular pets / by Mike Thaler; pictures
by Jerry Smath.
p.   cm.
"A Laffalong book"—T.p. verso.
Summary: Suggests using exotic pets like mooses, alligators, and
octopi, as hat racks, staplers, and string quartets.
ISBN 0-8167-3301-5 (lib. bdg.)   ISBN 0-8167-3302-3 (pbk.)
[1. Pets—Fiction.] I. Smath, Jerry, ill. II. Title.
PZ7.T3Us 1994

[E]—dc20   93-25542

Text copyright © 1994 by Mike Thaler.
Illustrations copyright © 1994 by Jerry Smath.
A LAFFALONG BOOK™ is a trademark of Mike Thaler.

Published by Troll Associates, Inc.
WhistleStop is a trademark of Troll Associates.

Printed in the United States of America.
10 9 8 7 6 5 4 3 2

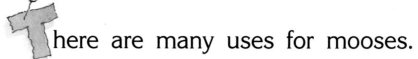

There are many uses for mooses.

For instance...

they make great hat racks,

Christmas trees,

and good left fielders.

They also make good beach chairs

and snow shovels.

Now, if you happen to have
a hippopotamus as a pet...

they make terrific trash cans,

book ends,

and baby carriages.

And, if you own an alligator...
they make fine hedge clippers,

staplers,

and musical instruments.

Most elephants make

good squirt guns…

and balloons, if you fill them
with helium.

Now, giraffes make super slides...

and help you to see parades!

While octopuses make
good traffic cops,

and string quartets.

And kangaroos make

good basketball hoops...

and letter carriers.

Beavers make good

Ping-Pong paddles,

coasters,

and serving trays.

You can send signals with rabbits,

use camels for couches,

and anteaters for vacuum cleaners.

You can use polar bears
for snowmen in summer,

monkeys for coat hangers
and umbrellas,

swordfish for darts...

and whales for drinking fountains.

So, as you can see,
there are many uses for mooses
and other popular pets,